# Great Americans

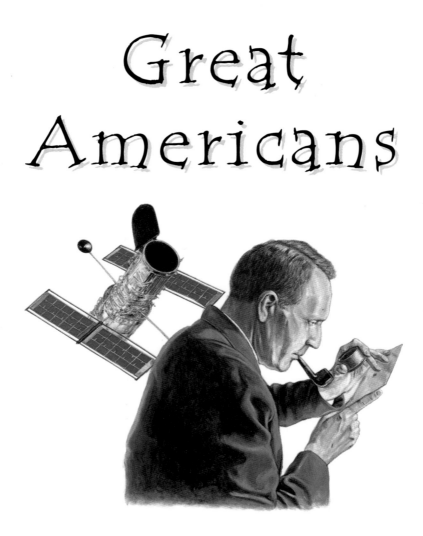

Written by Chris Oxlade
Illustrated by Adam Hook

p

This is a Parragon Publishing Book
This edition published in 2003

Parragon Publishing
Queen Street House
4 Queen Street
Bath BA1 1HE, UK

Copyright © Parragon 2000

ISBN 0-75259-872-4

Printed in China.

Produced by
Monkey Puzzle Media Ltd

# Contents

# Who is Uncle Sam?

NOBODY. UNCLE SAM IS A NICKNAME FOR THE UNITED STATES government. Nobody knows for certain the origin of the name, but it could have come from Samuel Wilson (1766—1854), an inspector of army supplies, who was nicknamed Uncle Sam.

## Who was the greatest president?

In 1962, a group of historians made a list of presidents in order of greatness. Top of the list was Abraham Lincoln (1809—1865). Lincoln was president during the Civil War (1861—1865), when the northern states (the Unionists), who wanted slavery abolished, fought the southern states (the Confederates), who wanted to keep it. Lincoln was assassinated soon after the Unionists had won victory.

Apart from being a great scientist, Franklin organized the first volunteer fire brigade and founded the first free public library.

## Which great statesman invented the lightning conductor?

Benjamin Franklin (1706—1790) signed the Declaration of Independence in 1776 as a representative of Pennsylvania. He also served as an ambassador to France, where he got French support for America's independence. Before his political career, Franklin worked as a scientist, mainly investigating electricity. He proved that lightning is caused by electricity and invented the lightning conductor.

### Who signed the Declaration of Independence?

On July 4, 1776, 13 British colonies declared themselves independent of Britain and formed the United States of America. Representatives from each of the colonies signed a document, named the Declaration of Independence. Among them were Benjamin Franklin, Thomas Jefferson (1743—1826), and John Hancock (1737—93).

### Which president won a Nobel Prize?

Woodrow Wilson (1856—1924), the 28th president of the United States. He was awarded the Nobel Prize for Peace in 1919 for his work in forming the League of Nations, the forerunner of the United Nations.

### Which American was the first woman Member of Parliament in Britain?

Nancy Witcher Langhorne (1879—1964) was born in Virginia. In 1906 she married Waldorf Astor and moved to England. In 1919 Nancy Astor was elected Member of Parliament for Plymouth, southern England. She served in Parliament until 1945.

### Which president was ambassador to Britain?

John Adams (1735—1826) was the first U.S. ambassador to Britain in 1785, two years after the United States' independence was recognized. Adams returned to the United States in 1788, to be elected vice president and then president (1797—1801).

### Who was the first president of the United States?

George Washington (1732—1799), who was elected president in 1789. Washington led the Continental army against the British during the American Revolution. He served two terms in office.

In his first year as Secretary of State, Kissinger signed the cease-fire agreement ending the Vietnam War.

### Which diplomat invented a shuttle?

Henry Kissinger (born 1923) was Secretary of State from 1973 to 1977. In 1974 he helped to arrange a cease-fire in the Arab-Israeli War by visiting and talking to each opposing side in turn. This became known as shuttle diplomacy.

# Who helped to warm the Cold War?

## WILLIAM A HARRIMAN (1891—1968) WAS A LONG-SERVING DIPLOMAT.

During World War II he was ambassador to the former Soviet Union, and in the 1960s he helped to negotiate the Nuclear Test-Ban Treaty.

## Who gave his life to abolish slavery?

Abolitionists were people who wanted to end slavery in the United States. In 1859 John Brown (1800—1859) made a plan to free slaves in the southern states. With 21 comrades he captured an arsenal of weapons at Harpers Ferry, Virginia. He was captured by troops and hanged a few days later. He kept up his antislavery position during his trial.

# Who were the suffragettes?

## SUFFRAGETTES WERE PEOPLE WHO

campaigned for equal rights for women. One of the most famous suffragettes in the United States was Elizabeth Cady Stanton (1815—1902), who was head of the National Woman's Suffrage Association. Lucretia Mott and Susan Anthony were other famous suffragettes.

Elizabeth Stanton based her ideas on the Declaration of Independence.

### Who was the first American saint?

Elizabeth Ann Seton (1774—1821) founded the Society for the Relief of Poor Widows with Small Children in 1797, and the Sisters of Charity in 1813. She was canonized (made a saint) in 1963.

### Which famous novelist was on the side of the poor?

Upton Sinclair (1878—1968) was a novelist who was also a socialist. He wrote about the exploitation of poor immigrant workers in industry, and campaigned for reforms. He won the Pulitzer Prize in 1943.

### Who was Jane Addams?

Jane Addams (1860—1935) was a social worker who fought against urban poverty in the United States. In 1889 she founded a famous community center in Chicago called Hull House. She shared the Nobel Prize for Peace in 1931.

### Who is the world's most famous preacher?

Baptist minister Billy Graham (born 1918) is the world's most famous evangelist. He has been organizing preaching tours since 1944. On a tour in 1949 he preached to a total of 350,000 people in Los Angeles and two million people in Madison Square Gardens, New York City.

### Who was an angel in battle?

The National Society of the Red Cross in the United States was founded in 1881 by Clara Barton (1821—1912). She was its president until 1904. As a nurse during the Civil War, Clara Barton was known as the "angel of the battlefield."

# Who had a dream?

MARTIN LUTHER KING (1929—1968) WAS A Baptist clergyman and leader in the civil rights movement, which campaigned for equal rights for black Americans in the 1950s and 1960s. In 1963 he made a famous speech. "I have a dream," he said, "that my four little children will one day live in a nation where they will not be judged by the color of their skin, but by the content of their character." Martin Luther King was assassinated in Memphis, Tennessee, in 1968.

### Who founded thousands of libraries?

Andrew Carnegie (1835—1919) was an industrialist who was born in Scotland and emigrated to the United States in 1848. He made a fortune in the steel business, which he used to build more than 2,800 public libraries worldwide.

Martin Luther King vowed to use "passive resistance and the weapon of love" to fight prejudice.

# Who led the Apaches?

COCHISE (1815—1874) LED HIS
APACHE WARRIORS
against the U.S. army in Arizona during the
1860s, after soldiers had killed his relatives.
Cochise finally surrendered in 1871.

### Who led the Union in the Civil War?
The two main men were Ulysses S. Grant (1822—
1885) and William Tecumseh Sherman (1820—1891).
Grant won several battles before becoming
commander-in-chief of all U.S. armies in
1864. Sherman was commander of
U.S. forces in the western area.

Cochise's revenge for
the deaths of his relatives was
so effective that troops, settlers and
traders all left the region.

### Who was Paul Revere?
Paul Revere (1735—1818) was a folk hero of the
American Revolution, during which the United States
won its independence from Britain. After a career as a
silversmith in Boston, Revere became a courier for the
rebels. In 1775 he rode from Boston to Lexington to
warn revolutionary leaders that British troops were on
the way. This journey was made famous in a poem by
Henry Longfellow called *Paul Revere's Ride*.

### Who led the Confederates?

Thomas Jonathan Jackson (1824—1863) and Robert E. Lee (1807—1870). "Stonewall" Jackson was a brigadier general in the Confederate army. He was accidentally shot dead by one of his own men. General Lee commanded the army of Northern Virginia.

### Who said: "Damn the torpedoes"?

David Glasgow Farragut (1801—1870) was a naval officer on the Union side in the Civil War. In 1864 his ships sailed to capture enemy forts in Mobile Bay, Alabama, which was protected by mines (called torpedoes at the time). Farragut sailed through the mines, crying: "Damn the torpedoes!"

### Which racing driver became an air ace?

By 1914 Eddie Rickenbacker (1890—1973) was one of the top racing drivers in the United States. He then joined the army, became an army pilot, and shot down 26 enemy planes during World War I. He eventually became president of Eastern Air Lines.

### Who is the U.S.S. *Nimitz* named after?

U.S.S. *Nimitz* is one of the largest aircraft carriers in the world. It is named after Admiral Chester William Nimitz (1885—1966). Nimitz served in submarines in World War I and was commander of U.S. naval forces in the Pacific in World War II.

### Which naval hero was killed in a duel?

Stephen Decatur (1779—1820) was the naval officer who led a raid on Tripoli harbor, in Libya, in 1804 to destroy a captured U.S. ship. He was awarded the sword of honor. Decatur was killed in a duel with a fellow officer.

Eisenhower became president in 1953 and remained in power for eight years.

# Who led the U.S. in World War II?

DWIGHT D. EISENHOWER (1890—1969) JOINED THE ARMY DURING WORLD War I and served until 1948. In 1943, during World War II, he became a general and was given the title of Supreme Allied Commander. He was ordered to plan the Allied invasion of Europe, Operation Overlord, which began with the D-day landings in France on June 6, 1944.

The Model-T was known as "the motor car for the multitude."

# Who got rich with sleeping?

IN 1859 GEORGE MORTIMER PULLMAN (1831—1897) STARTED UP A BUSINESS converting regular railroad cars into luxury sleeping cars. His Pullman Palace Car Company made him a fortune, with which he built a town, now part of Chicago. "Pullman" is now used to describe any luxury railroad carriage.

### Who made a fortune from software?

Bill Gates (born 1955) is the man that founded Microsoft, the company which created the operating systems MS-DOS and Windows. These programs are now used on almost every PC in the world. Gates left university early to start Microsoft with a friend, and became a billionaire in 1986 when the company was floated on the stock market.

### Who started an industry with a Model-T?

The Model-T was the first mass-produced car. It was made by the Ford Motor Company, which was started in 1903 by Henry Ford (1863—1947). More than 15 million Model-Ts were made and sold.

### Who got rich by keeping warm?

John Jacob Astor (1763—1848) was born in Germany and emigrated to the United States with no money. He started with a small shop in New York City selling furs and built up the American Fur Company. He became the richest man in the U.S.

### Who got rich by staying cold?

Clarence Birdseye (1886—1956) was an inventor who started the frozen food industry. One of his experiments was to try to keep food fresh for long periods by freezing it. The freezing process he developed kept the flavor of the food while it was frozen.

# Who founded a ten-cent store?

**FRANK WINFIELD WOOLWORTH (1852—1919) OPENED HIS FIRST** store in Lancaster, Pennsylvania, in 1879. Everything on sale cost five or ten cents. By 1910 more than 1,000 Woolworth stores had opened worldwide.

In 1913 Frank Winfield Woolworth built the Woolworth Building in New York City. At the time it was the world's tallest building at 792 ft (241 m) high.

### What did Harvey Firestone make?
Firestone is a name that might appear on your car. Harvey Firestone (1868—1938) began manufacturing rubber tires for motor vehicles in 1896. The Firestone Fire and Rubber Company became one of top tire makers in the world.

### Who founded the New York Tribune?
The New York Tribune is one of the city's great newspapers. It was started in 1841 by Horace Greeley (1811—1872), who edited it for 30 years. In its early years, the Tribune was famous for its articles against slavery.

### Which oil man loved art?
John Paul Getty (1892—1976) became a billionaire from oil. He was probably the richest man in the world when he died. In 1953 he founded the John Paul Getty Museum in Malibu where his art collection is shown. In 1982 the museum founded the John Paul Getty Trust to help artists.

# Who disappeared while flying around the world?

AMELIA EARHART (1897—1937) WAS A PIONEERING AVIATOR. IN 1932 she became the first woman to fly nonstop across the Atlantic Ocean solo and to fly nonstop from coast to coast across the United States. In 1937 she attempted to fly around the world with copilot Frederick Noonan. Their aircraft disappeared after leaving New Guinea. It was never found.

Amelia's plane is thought to have gone down off the coast of Howland Island, near Honolulu.

### Who was the first person to find the North Pole?
Robert Edwin Peary (1856—1920) was an explorer who made several expeditions to the Arctic around the turn of the century. On April 6, 1909, he became first person to reach the North Pole.

### Who flew around the world alone?
Wiley Post (1899—1935) was a pilot who set many aviation records. In 1933 he flew around the world solo in a Lockheed Vega aircraft in just under eight days. Post was killed in a plane crash.

### Who made the first solo flight over the Atlantic Ocean?
Charles Lindburgh (1902—1974) made his flight in his aircraft *Spirit of St Louis* on May 20—21, 1927. The flight between New York and Paris, France took 33 hours and 39 minutes. Lindburgh's main problem was staying awake.

### Who was the first American to fly around the Earth in space?

Lieutenant Colonel John Glenn made three orbits of the Earth in a Friendship capsule launched by a Mercury rocket on February 20, 1962. The flight lasted nearly five hours.

### Which around-the-world sailor could not swim?

Joshua Slocum (1844—1910) spent most of his life at sea. In 1898, after retiring as a ship's captain, he set out in an old fishing boat named *Spray* to become the first yachtsman to sail around the world solo. But Slocum could not swim and disappeared at sea with *Spray* in 1910.

### Who led an expedition to the West?

The Lewis and Clark expedition set out in 1804 to explore overland to the Pacific coast of America. In charge was Captain Meriwether Lewis (1774—1809). The explorers returned two and half years later having covered 8,000 miles (13,000 km).

### Who helped found the American Geographical Society?

Adolphus Washington Greely (1844—1935). From 1881 to 1883 Greely carried out an exploration of Greenland that ended in tragedy when all but six of his 25 men died of hunger during the winter.

### Which bird flew over the North Pole in 1924?

Richard Evelyn Byrd (1888—1957) was a naval flier and explorer. In 1926 he became the first person to fly over the North Pole. Byrd also made five expeditions to the Antarctic and set up a U.S. Antarctic base.

When Apollo 11 landed on the Moon the astronauts said "The Eagle has landed."

# Who made a giant leap for mankind?

On July 21, 1969, the lunar module of Apollo 11 landed on the Moon. Its commander Neil Alden Armstrong (born 1930) was the first man to step onto the Moon's surface, saying: "This is one small step for man, one giant leap for mankind." His fellow astronaut Buzz Aldrin followed him down the ladder.

Disney's first theme park, Disneyland, opened in California in 1955.

### Which actress has won the most Oscars?
Katherine Hepburn (born 1907) has won most Oscars in the Best Actress category, with four from 13 nominations. She was awarded her first for *Morning Glory* (1933) and her last for *On Golden Pond* (1981) when she was 74.

### Which man with a girl's name played tough cowboys?
Marion Michael Morrison, better known as John Wayne (1906—1979), and often called simply "Duke," was famous for playing tough cowboys and soldiers in westerns and war films. He appeared in more than 150 feature films. His first major role was as the Ringo Kid in *Stagecoach* in 1939. He was presented with an Academy Award in 1969 for the part of Rooster Cogburn in *True Grit.*

### Who are the great American film directors?
A difficult question! Everybody will have their favorite. Some of the big names to look up are Frank Capra (1897—1991), Howard Hawks (1896—1977), John Ford (1895—1973), Stanley Kubrick (1928—1999), Francis Ford Coppola (born 1939), George Lucas (born 1945), and Steven Spielberg (born 1946).

### What sort of show did Barnum run?
A circus. Phineas Taylor Barnum (1810—1891) was a showman who opened his own circus in 1871. Modestly, he named it "The Greatest Show on Earth." In 1881 he joined forces with a rival to form the famous Barnum and Bailey Circus.

# Who invented a cartoon mouse?

THE MAN WHO STARTED DISNEY FILMS, WALTER ELIAS (WALT) DISNEY (1901—1966). In 1928 Walt Disney invented the character Mickey Mouse and made the first Mickey Mouse movie, *Steamboat Willie*. Disney released *Snow White and the Seven Dwarfs*, the first feature-length animated movie, in 1938.

# Who was Buffalo Bill?

**Who is America's most popular talk show host?**
Oprah Winfrey (born 1954), who is known to most viewers simply as Oprah. She began her career as a news presenter for CBS at 19. The Oprah Winfrey Show started in 1986.

BUFFALO BILL'S REAL NAME WAS WILLIAM Frederick Cody (1846—1917). He was a scout for the U.S. army and a buffalo hunter. In 1883 he started Buffalo Bill's Wild West Show, which toured towns and cities across the U.S., with exhibitions of hunting, riding, and shooting.

**Who are America's greatest actors?**
Pick from Marlon Brando (born 1924), Humphrey Bogart (1899 —1957), Henry Fonda (1905—1982), John Wayne (1907—1979), Katherine Hepburn (born 1907), Bette Davis (1908—1989), James Stewart (1908—1997), Jane Fonda (born 1937), Dustin Hoffman (born 1937), Robert de Niro (born 1943), Meryl Streep (born 1949), Tom Hanks (born 1956), or Michelle Pfeiffer (born 1957). Or choose your own!

**Which newscaster was the face of CBS?**
Walter Cronkite (born 1916) came to fame as a CBS newscaster. Between 1962 and 1981 he was anchorman of the CBS evening news program. His face became known in every U.S. home.

**Which magician escaped from everything?**
Harry Houdini (1874—1926), real name Erich Weiss. Houdini became world famous as a magician and escapologist. His trademark trick was to escape from a sealed container full of water after being handcuffed and put in a straitjacket.

Houdini was born in Hungary but lived in the United States.

## What did Ernest Hemingway write about?

Ernest Hemingway (1889—1961) was one of the greatest American writers. He wrote novels—about brave people living dangerous lives, especially during wars—such as *A Farewell to Arms* (1929) and *For Whom the Bell Tolls* (1940).

Hemingway's novel *The Old Man and the Sea* won him the Nobel prize for literature in 1954.

## Who went with the wind?

Margaret Mitchell (1900—1949) wrote only one novel, and it took her 10 years to complete. But it became one of the most famous novels of all time. It was *Gone with the Wind*, a story about a family in Georgia during and after the Civil War. It was published in 1936 and became an instant bestseller. It was made into an even more famous film of the same name in 1939.

## Who wrote Little Women?

LOUISA MAY ALCOTT (1832—1888) WAS A NURSE DURING THE CIVIL WAR. SHE completed her most famous book, *Little Women*, in 1869. It is about life in an American family during the 1800s.

## Who wrote Uncle Tom's Cabin?

*Uncle Tom's Cabin* was the first antislavery novel to be published in the United States. It was written in 1852 by Harriet Beecher Stowe (1811—1896) and became a very popular book and play. It helped the antislavery cause before the Civil War.

## Who are the greatest poets of the U.S?

Difficult to say! Two of the best are Walt Whitman (1819—1892) and Henry Wadsworth Longfellow (1807—1882). Whitman was a Civil War nurse and wrote war poetry. Longfellow was a popular poet who wrote *Paul Revere's Ride*.

# Who was Huckleberry Finn?

Huckleberry Finn was a fictional character in the book the *Adventures of Huckleberry Finn*, published in 1884. It was written by Mark Twain (1835—1910), one of the greatest writers in the U.S. Twain's real name was Samuel Longhorn Clemens. Before becoming a writer, Twain worked as a boat pilot on the Mississippi River. His other famous novels include *The Prince and the Pauper* (1882) and *The Adventures of Tom Sawyer* (1876).

## Whose first success was *The Glass Menagerie*?

*The Glass Menagerie* was written in 1944 by playwright Tennessee Williams (1914—1983). Williams wrote about the difficulties of life. Another famous play of his, *A Streetcar Named Desire*, won him a Pulitzer Prize.

Marlon Brando played the lead role in a film version of *A Streetcar Named Desire*.

## Which writer campaigned for civil rights?

James Baldwin (1924—1987) was a black American who wrote books, shorts stories, and plays about black Americans and race relations in the United States. In the 1950s he campaigned for civil rights for blacks.

## Who was the first writer from the United States to win a Nobel Prize?

In 1930 Sinclair Lewis (1885—1951) became the first American to win a Nobel Prize for Literature. He wrote novels about the lives of middle-class Americans.

## Whose most famous book is *The Grapes of Wrath*?

It was written in 1939 by John Steinbeck (1902—1968). It is a story about poor farmers living through a terrible drought in the 1930s.. Steinbeck won the Nobel Prize for Literature in 1962.

Frank Sinatra died in 1998 after a career spanning nearly 60 years.

## Which singer was the King?

"The King" was the nickname of the great rock and roll singer Elvis Presley (1935—1977). He was also known as "Elvis the Pelvis" because of the way he moved his hips while he sang. As a teenager, Presley lived in Memphis, where he listened to rhythm and blues music. He came to fame in the mid-1950s with a new style of rock and roll music. He made 45 records, which sold more than a million copies. He also appeared in 33 films.

## Which brothers wrote Broadway musicals?

George Gershwin (1898—1937) and Ira Gershwin (1896—1983) teamed up to write several Broadway musicals, including *Porgy and Bess*. George composed the musical scores and Ira wrote the lyrics.

## Who was America's greatest singer?

Most people would say Frank Sinatra. He started his singing career in the mid-1930s and was world famous by the early 1940s, when he also started acting. He won an Oscar in 1953 for his role in *From Here to Eternity*.

## Which rock and roll singer died aged 22?

Buddy Holly (1936—1959), whose real name was Charles Harden Holly. He was a singer, songwriter, and guitarist, who made several hit records with his group The Crickets in the 1950s. He was killed in a plane crash.

# Who wrote "God Bless America"?

RUSSIAN-BORN SONGWRITER ISRAEL BALINE (1888—1989) MOVED TO the United States as a boy. When his first song was published, the printer had spelt his name Irving Berlin, so he named himself that. Irving Berlin became perhaps the greatest songwriter in the United States. He wrote nearly 800 songs, including *God Bless America*, and dozens of Broadway shows, including *Annie Get Your Gun*.

## Who composed military marches?

John Philip Sousa (1854—1932). Between 1880 and 1892 Sousa was leader of the band of the U.S. Marines. He wrote more than 100 tunes for military marches, including *The Stars and Stripes Forever*.

## Which jazz player was a "Count"?

"Count" Basie (1904—1984) was not a real count. His proper name was William Basie. His nickname was thought up by a radio station presenter. Basie was a top jazz pianist and band leader.

## Who invented the Jets and the Sharks?

The Jets and the Sharks were two gangs of youths in the musical *West Side Story*. It was one of the musicals written by Leonard Bernstein (1918—1990), a conductor and composer.

Madonna is now the most photographed woman in the world.

# Is Madonna the star's real name?

YES, HER FULL NAME IS MADONNA LOUISE CICCONE AND SHE GREW UP IN Pontiac, Michigan, a suburb of Detroit. Her father immigrated from Italy and her mother is French Canadian.

**Who was Satchmo?**

The jazz singer and trumpet player Louis Armstrong (1900—1971). Armstrong began singing in New Orleans as a teenager and became probably the most influential jazz musician of all time.

Frank Lloyd Wright was one of the most important figures in Western architecture.

### Which artist painted in London ... at night?

James Whistler (1834—1903) spent most of his working life outside the United States. He moved to Paris, France in 1855 and to London in 1859. During the 1870s he painted several famous pictures of London, England at night.

# Who designed a mile-high skyscraper?

### Who is famous for dripping paint?

Jackson Pollock (1912—1956) painted abstract pictures that revealed his feelings on the canvas instead of showing scenes of the real world. He often used the technique of dripping swirling lines of paint on to a huge canvas, which he called "action painting."

## FRANK LLOYD WRIGHT (1869—1959) WAS A FAMOUS AMERICAN ARCHITECT

who created extraordinary new styles of architecture. One of his most famous designs is the Guggenheim Museum in New York. Wright also designed many buildings that were never built, including a "mile-high" skyscraper, which would have been three times higher than the highest modern skyscrapers.

### What did Buckminster Fuller invent?

Buckminster Fuller (1895—1983) was an architect and engineer who came up with several new ideas for building shapes. One of these was called the geodesic dome, which is a domed building made of a framework of triangles.

### Who painted birds?

The ornithologist and artist John James Audubon (1785—1851) made a detailed study of the native birds of the United States. In 1838 he published *The Birds of America*, a book of paintings and drawings of all the birds.

### Who was the first great portrait painter of the United States?

John Singleton Copley (1738—1815) was the greatest portrait painter of his time. He worked in Boston, New York City, Philadelphia, and London, England. His portraits included those of revolutionary hero Paul Revere and politician Samuel Adams.

### Who is famous for sculpting people?

Poor eyesight prevented Sir Jacob Epstein (1880—1959) from being a painter. Instead he turned to sculpting, and became brilliant at creating figures of people. Epstein was born in New York City, and set up a studio in London, England, in 1905.

# Who painted soup cans?

THE ARTIST ANDY WARHOL (1928—1987). HE WAS ONE OF THE LEADERS OF A group of artists who started a new style of art called "pop art" in the early 1960s. The artists used everyday objects to make up their pictures. Warhol's most famous paintings are made up of lots of images of the same object, such as soup cans, in strange colors.

### What did Ansel Adams do?

Ansel Adams (1902—1984) was a photographer. He took superb black-and-white photographs of landscapes, especially of the southwest of the United States. He also wrote many books on photographic technique.

Andy Warhol was not just an artist, he was also involved in film-making, photography, and publishing.

From the age of 12, Einstein was determined to solve "the riddle of the world."

**Who worked out that E=mc² ?**
A man with one of the greatest scientific minds of all time, Albert Einstein (1879—1955). Einstein was a theoretical physicist. He was born in Germany, moved to the United States in 1940, and became an American citizen. His most famous works are his Special Theory of Relativity (1905) and General Theory of Relativity (1916). Part of the special theory stated that mass (m) can be changed into energy (E) according to the equation $E=mc^2$.

**Who encouraged education?**
Two of America's leading educationalists were Nicholas Murray Butler (1862—1947), who shared the Nobel Prize for Peace in 1931, and John Dewey (1859—1952), who lectured all over the world on education.

**Whose name appears on every library book?**
Melvil Dewey (1851—1931) was a famous librarian. He invented a system of classifying books by their subject named Dewey decimal. All library books have a Dewey number.

# Who started a detective agency?

ALLAN PINKERTON (1819—1884) WAS IN CHARGE OF ARMY SPIES ON THE Union side during the Civil War. In 1850 he started a private detective agency in Chicago, which became the famous Pinkerton National Detective Agency.

# Which mathematician took polls?

GEORGE HORACE GALLUP (1901—1984)
WAS A STATISTICIAN WHO
developed the Gallup Poll for judging public opinion on subjects. The poll is taken by asking a random selection of people simple questions.

**What did Noah Webster write?**
Books on the English language, including spelling and grammar. Noah Webster (1758—1843) was a lexicographer (a writer of dictionaries). In 1812 he completed *The American Dictionary of English Language*.

Bobby Fischer had an incredibly high I.Q. He was the youngest grandmaster in the history of chess, at 15.

**Who are America's famous economists?**
Milton Friedman (born 1912) and John Kenneth Galbraith (born 1908). Friedman was professor at the University of Chicago and won the 1976 Nobel Prize for Economics. Galbraith taught at Harvard and was U.S. ambassador to India in the 1960s.

**Who was famous for checkmates?**
The chess player Bobby Fischer (born 1943). Fischer started playing when he was six and won the American Championship at 15. In 1972 he won the World Championship in one of the most famous chess matches of all time. His opponent was Soviet player Boris Spassky. The match took place during the Cold War, and was seen as a battle between capitalism and communism.

# Who has a telescope named after him?

Edwin Powell Hubble (1889—1953), the famous astronomer who was the first person to show that the universe is made up of huge groups of stars called galaxies with space between them. Hubble also showed that the universe is getting bigger and bigger. He did most of his work at Mount Wilson Observatory, California. The Hubble Space Telescope that orbits the Earth is named after him.

Hubble originally studied law, but he changed his mind and studied astronomy. He became one of the finest astronomers of the modern world.

## Who helped to build a nuclear bomb?

In 1942 nuclear scientist Robert J. Oppenheimer (1904—1967) became director of the Los Alamos laboratory in New Mexico. Here scientists created the world's first atomic bomb.

## Who was the first woman to become a doctor?

Elizabeth Blackwell (1821—1910) was born in England and moved to the United States in 1832. In 1849 she graduated from Geneva Medical College, New York, to become the first woman in the United States to get a medical degree.

### What did Albert Michelson measure?

The speed of light. Albert Michelson (1852—1931) was a physicist who built a device called an interferometer, which he used to measure the speed of light far more accurately than it had been measured before. In 1907 he received the Nobel Prize for Physics.

### Who discovered Barnard's Star?

No surprise here! It was the astronomer Edward Emerson Barnard (1857—1923). In 1916 Barnard discovered a star that is moving very quickly compared to the other stars. It is now called Barnard's star. Barnard also discovered 16 comets and a moon of Jupiter.

### Who was a famous brain surgeon?

Harvey Williams Cushing (1869—1939). He was the first person to describe the medical syndrome (abnormality) that is now called Cushing's syndrome.

Pauling was the man who found the cause of the disease, sickle cell anaemia.

### Who is the only man to win two Nobel prizes?

Linus Carl Pauling (1901—1994) was a brilliant chemist. He was awarded his first Nobel Prize (for chemistry) in 1954. In 1962 Pauling was awarded the Nobel Prize for Peace for his campaign against nuclear weapons testing.

# Who modeled DNA?

DNA IS A CHEMICAL THAT HOLDS THE CODE FOR HOW ALL ANIMALS

and plants grow and live. The way the chemical's atoms are joined together was first modeled in 1953 by biologists James Dewey Watson (born 1928) from the United States and Francis Crick (born 1916) from Britain.

## Who made rubber useful?

A process named vulcanization makes rubber last longer and makes it stay rubbery when it is very hot or very cold. The process was invented by Charles Goodyear (1800—1860) in 1839, and it allowed long-lasting vehicle tires to be made.

## Who got the sewing machine going?

Isaac Merritt Singer (1811—1875). He marketed the first sewing machine for home use, which was patented in 1851. The Singer became a worldwide best seller. The sewing machine was actually invented in France in 1829 by Barthélemy Thimmonier.

## Who invented a famous code?

Samuel Finley Breese Morse (1791—1872) was an inventor and a pioneer of the electric telegraph—a device for sending messages along wires. Morse invented a code of dots and dashes that represent letters and numbers. It is known as Morse code.

## What did Chester Floyd Carlson copy?

Anything written on paper—he invented xerography (now called photocopying) in 1938. Chester Floyd Carlson (1906—1968) founded a company that is now the Xerox Corporation.

# Who said: "Come in here, Watson"?

## The inventor of the telephone,

Alexander Graham Bell (1847—1922). Bell was born in Scotland. He was interested in speech therapy, and taught people with hearing difficulties how to speak at a school in Boston. In 1876 he demonstrated an invention that allowed speech to be sent along a wire—the telephone. His first words on his telephone were: "Come in here, Watson," spoken to his assistant, who was in the next room.

The first name for the telephone was the "electric speech machine."

### Which brothers built the first airplane?

The Wright brothers — Orville (1871—1948) and Wilbur (1867—1912). In December 1903, at Kitty Hawk, North Carolina, their home-built plane *Flyer* made the first proper controlled flight by a powered aircraft.

### How did Robert Hutchings Goddard rocket to fame?

He was a builder of rockets. In 1926 Robert Hutchings Goddard (1882—1945) developed the first rocket fueled by liquids rather than solid fuel.

### Who made elevators safe?

In 1852 Elisha Graves Otis (1811—1861) invented a safety device that stopped goods elevators falling to the ground if the rope broke. This allowed safe passenger elevators to be developed.

### Which telegraph operator invented light bulbs?

Thomas Alva Edison (1847—1931) was probably the greatest inventor of all. He worked as telegraph operator on the American railroads during the 1860s, where he got the idea for a new type of telegraph machine. He also invented a light bulb, the microphone and the phonograph, which was the forerunner of the record player.

# Who helped us to take holiday snaps?

GEORGE EASTMAN (1854—1932) WAS A PIONEER OF PHOTOGRAPHY. IN 1888 he developed the first simple camera that was sold to the public, the Kodak camera. It was loaded with film that the owner could send off for processing.

Martina Navratilova was born in 1956 in Czechoslovakia, and by the age of 17 she had been national champion three times. She became a U.S. citizen in 1981, and then won 18 Grand Slam singles titles, including a record nine at Wimbledon, England.

**Who started life as
Cassius Clay?**
The heavyweight boxer Muhammad Ali (born 1942). He was born as Cassius Clay, and changed his name in 1964 after becoming a Muslim. Ali was the only boxer to win the heavyweight world championship three times, in 1964, 1974, and 1978. He won 56 of his 61 professional fights. Ali proclaimed himself as *The Greatest*, and made up raplike poems about himself.

Peter Sampras is rated the number one tennis player in the world.

**Who ran to fame
in 1936?**
The sprinter Jesse Owens (1913—1980). Owens' real name was James Cleveland, and his initials JC were turned into Jesse by his school teacher. At 22, he set four world sprinting and jumping records in the space of 45 minutes. At the 1936 Olympics in Berlin, Owens won four gold medals — the 100 meters, the 200 meters, the long jump, and the sprint relay.

# Which tennis tournament has Pete Sampras not won?

D ESPITE HIS GREAT CAREER SUCCESS, SAMPRAS HAS NEVER GOT further than the semifinals in the French Open. The games are played on red clay courts and Sampras does not enjoy playing on them and sees the Open as a major challenge.

**Who was the greatest all-around athlete?**
At the 1912 Stockholm Olympics, Sweden, where Jim Thorpe (1888—1953) won both the pentathlon and decathlon, the King of Sweden said to him: "Sir, you are the greatest athlete in the world." Thorpe also played professional baseball and football.

# Who was named Golfer of the Century?

## IN 1988 THE PROFESSIONAL GOLF ASSOCIATION OF THE

United States named Jack Nicklaus (born 1940) Golfer of the Century. He became a professional golfer in 1961, and a year later became youngest player to win the U.S. Open, the first of his 20 championship wins.

### Who is the greatest quarterback?

Joe Montana (born 1956) dominated the National Football League during the 1980s playing for the San Francisco 49ers. With Montana in command, they won the Super Bowl four times, three times with Montana as Most Valuable Player.

### Who swam to seven Olympic golds?

At the 1972 Olympics in Munich, U.S. swimmer Mark Spitz (born 1950) made history by winning seven gold medals, four in individual events and three in relays.

### What is The House that Ruth Built?

Yankee Stadium, home of the New York Yankees baseball team. It got its nickname from Babe Ruth (1895—1948), the greatest baseball batter of all time, who played in it throughout the 1920s. He hit a record 714 home runs in his career.

### Who is "Magic" on a basketball court?

The basketball player Earvin "Magic" Johnson (born 1959). For the Los Angeles Lakers, Johnson was Most Valuable Player, three times as the Lakers won five NBA titles. He played in the U.S. Dream Team at the 1992 Olympics, despite being diagnosed HIV positive in 1991.

### What did the Kennedy brothers do?

There were three brothers in the most famous political family in the United States. Their father was Joseph Patrick Kennedy (1888—1969). John Fitzgerald Kennedy (1917—1963) was inaugurated as president in 1961, and assassinated in 1963. Robert Francis Kennedy (1925—1968) was attorney general, and was assassinated in 1968 while running for president. Edward Moore Kennedy (born 1932) is a senator.

### Who were the Rockefellers?

The Rockefellers are a family of entrepreneurs. John Davison Rockefeller (1839—1937) made a huge fortune in oil refining. His son John D. Rockefeller (1874—1960), built the Rockefeller Center in New York City, and his son, Nelson Rockefeller (1908—1970), was vice president from 1974 to 1977.

### How did Laurel meet Hardy?

Stan Laurel (1890—1965) and Oliver Hardy (1892—1957) were a comedy duo who made nearly 90 slapstick films. The two men joined a film studio separately in 1926, and the studio owner persuaded them to team up.

### What did Rodgers and Hammerstein write?

Oscar Hammerstein (1895—1960) wrote the lyrics to many musicals, and often teamed up with the composer Richard Rodgers (1902—1979). Together they created famous musicals such as *Oklahoma!* and *The King and I*.

# Who founded their own museum?

THE GUGGENHEIMS ARE A FAMILY OF INDUSTRIALISTS. MEYER Guggenheim (1828—1905) emigrated from Switzerland in 1847 and had seven sons. One of the seven, Simon Guggenheim (1861—1949) started a foundation that helped artists and writers. Another, Solomon Robert Guggenheim, started a foundation that built the famous Guggenheim Museum in New York City.